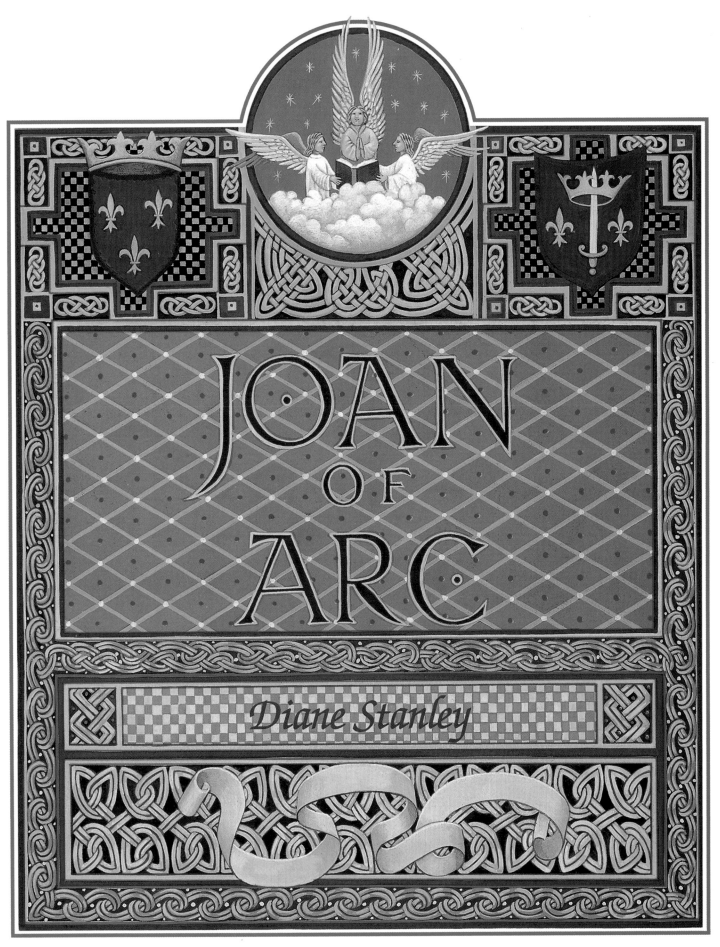

JOAN OF ARC

Diane Stanley

HarperCollins*Publishers*

The author wishes to thank Dr. Katherine F. Drew, Professor of
History Emeritus at Rice University, for her careful reading of the text.

For Emily Jennings Ivey

Acrylics were used for the full-color illustrations.
The text type is 13.5-point Centaur MT.

Joan of Arc
Copyright © 1998 by Diane Stanley
Manufactured in China. All rights reserved.

Library of Congress Cataloging-in-Publication Data
Stanley, Diane.
Joan of Arc / Diane Stanley.
p.   cm.
Includes bibliographical references.
Summary: A biography of the fifteenth-century
peasant girl who led a French army to victory against
the English and was burned at the stake for witchcraft.
ISBN 0-688-14329-6 (trade) — ISBN 0-688-14330-X (lib. bdg.)
ISBN 0-06-443748-5 (pbk.)
1. Joan, of Arc, Saint, 1412–1431—Juvenile literature.
2. Christian saints—France—Biography—Juvenile literature.
3. France—History—Charles VII, 1422–1461—Juvenile literature.
[1. Joan, of Arc, Saint, 1412–1431.   2. Saints.   3. Women—Biography.
4. France—History—Charles VII, 1422–1461.]   I. Title.   DC103.5.S66
1998   940'.026'092—dc21   [B]   97-45652   CIP   AC

Visit us on the World Wide Web!
www.harperchildrens.com

A Hundred Years of War

Imagine your country is at war. The fighting is not at some faraway place but right where you live. From time to time, soldiers march into your town, killing people and taking whatever they want. They might burn your house or even the whole town. There's not enough food to eat, because the enemy has taken or destroyed the crops. But you're used to it, because you have never known what it is like to live in peace. Neither have your parents or your grandparents. In fact, the war has been going on since your great-great-grandparents were children. Sometimes it doesn't seem to matter who wins. Soon there will be nothing left to fight for. That was what life was like in France during the Hundred Years' War.

The war began in 1337, when the English king claimed that France should rightfully be part of England. This was not as outrageous as it sounds, since over the course of the previous three hundred years the two countries had become deeply connected through many royal marriages. The true line of succession had become tangled and confusing. The English, convinced their claim was just, invaded France. The French, naturally, did not want to be part of England and fought valiantly to drive the English out. The two countries would go on fighting about it, off and on, until 1453. This was a war that truly deserved its name.

Since this was the Middle Ages, the people of France couldn't follow events in the newspaper, but word spread quickly when anything important happened. Around 1392, some fifty years into the war, they began to hear rumors that their king, Charles VI, had fallen into spells of madness and that his uncle was running things for him. This uncle, known as Philip the Good, was the duke of Burgundy, an important and powerful man, richer even than the king. The duke thought it was better to let the English have their way than to go on fighting year after year. Queen Isabeau agreed, and in 1420 she convinced the mad king to sign a treaty and make peace. Having helped to arrange all this, the duke of Burgundy was assured that he would have even more power in the new France.

The agreement was that Charles VI would go on ruling France until his death, but thereafter both countries would be ruled by the English king. To make this more acceptable to the French, Henry V of England married the French princess, Catherine. If all went well, they would produce an heir who was half French and half English.

It looked as if the war would finally end, but there was one important person who refused to go along with the treaty. That was Catherine's teenage brother, Charles. He was the crown prince, or dauphin, which meant he was the rightful heir to the French throne. Now he had been rudely shoved aside. His mother had even implied that he didn't deserve to rule because he wasn't really the king's son. Considering Isabeau's bad reputation and the king's mental illness, many people believed it.

But others took Charles's side. They wanted a real French dauphin to rule after the king. These people hated Queen Isabeau and the duke of Burgundy, too, for handing over France to the enemy.

The final blow to peace came two years later, when the king of France died. As fate would have it, Henry V could not succeed him as planned, for he had died two months before. This left two claimants to the throne of France. One was Henry VI, the nine-month-old son of Henry V and his French bride, Catherine. The other, of course, was the dauphin, Charles VII, who was only nineteen. The forces supporting each of them divided France in two, with the English and Burgundians controlling the north and the French holding the territory south of the Loire River. If there's anything worse than foreign occupation, it's civil war. Now the French were not only fighting the English, they were also fighting each other.

The French cause looked grim. The dauphin was young and inexperienced, his treasury depleted. Even if he could find the money to pay his army, there was little hope of winning.

And then the miracle occurred. It came not from the halls of wealth and power but from a remote and humble village called Domremy. From that unexpected place an illiterate peasant girl, still in her teens, set out on a quest that would change the course of history. She had been born around 1412, though we don't know the exact date for sure. Peasants in those days did not keep records, and few of them knew their own age. Her parents, a farmer and his wife, named her Jeannette. We know her as Joan of Arc.

Pronunciation Guide

Prepared by Janet Vrancken of St. John's School, Houston, Texas

Look at the French word on the left and then read the pronunciation on the right as if it were an English word. Note, however, that there are no emphasized syllables in French.

Say *j* as if it were the letter *s* in *pleasure.*

M and *n* after certain vowels are not really pronounced at all in French. To say these sounds, imagine you have a bad cold and your nose is blocked; now say *n* or *m.* You will see a triangle (▲) after the vowel to indicate that you need to use this sound.

a blanc	a blo▲	Jeanne	jan
Alençon	a-lo▲-so▲	Jeannette	jan-et
Augustins	oh-gew-sta▲	La Hire	la eer
beau duc	boh dewk	La Pucelle	la pew-sel
Beaugency	boh-jo▲-see	Loire	lwar
Beauvais	boh-vay	Orléans	or-lay-o▲
Chinon	shee-no▲	Pierre Cauchon	pee-air koh-sho▲
Compiègne	kom-pee-en-yuh	Poitiers	pwat-ee-ay
dauphin	doh-fa▲	Reims	ra▲s
Domremy	do▲-ray-mee	Robert de Baudricourt	ro-bair duh boh-dree-koor
Dunois	dew-nwa	Rouen	roo-o▲
Durand Laxart	dew-ro▲ laks-ar	Saint-Denis	sa▲-duh-nee
Fierbois	fee-air-bwa	Saint-Loup	sa▲-loo
Isabeau	ee-za-boh	Saint-Ouen	sa▲-too-o▲
Jacques d'Arc	jak dark	Seine	sayn
Jargeau	jar-joh	Tourelles	too-rel
Jean Lemaître	jo▲ luh-maytr	Vaucouleurs	voh-koo-ler

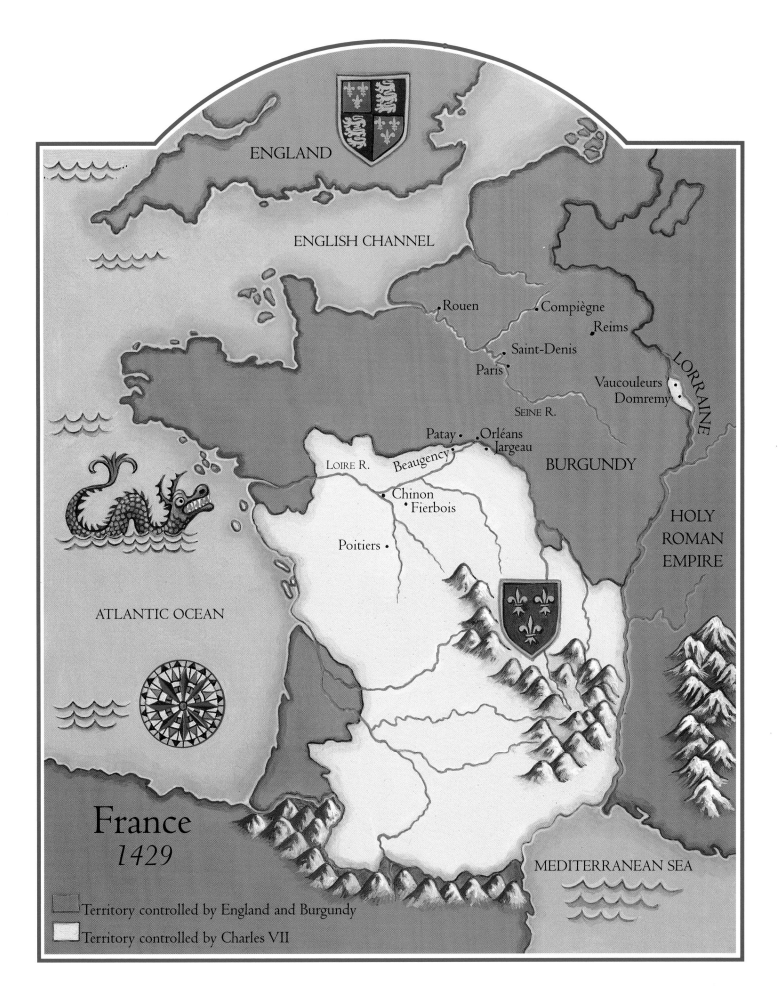

ENGLAND

ENGLISH CHANNEL

Rouen

Compiègne

Reims

Saint-Denis

Paris

Vaucouleurs
Domremy

LORRAINE

SEINE R.

Patay
Orléans
Jargeau

Beaugency

LOIRE R.

BURGUNDY

Chinon
Fierbois

HOLY
ROMAN
EMPIRE

Poitiers

ATLANTIC OCEAN

France
1429

MEDITERRANEAN SEA

Territory controlled by England and Burgundy

Territory controlled by Charles VII

The future savior of France was much like all the other little girls in the village of Domremy. She was an ordinary peasant child, sunburned and strong, used to hard work. Sometimes she helped her father out in the fields or in the garden. On other days, she looked after the animals. But mostly, she stayed at home with her mother and did housework. She was especially proud of her skill at spinning and sewing.

Jacques d'Arc, Joan's father, was something of a leader in the village, and the family lived in a stone house next door to the church. But do not imagine anything grand. It had a dirt floor, and the rooms were musty and damp. There were no bathrooms, and no one in the village was likely to be very clean.

Her mother and father were strict with their five children, raising them to be good Catholics. Like her parents, Joan could neither read nor write. The only education she ever had was from her mother, Isabelle, who taught all the children to say their prayers and to understand the teachings of the Church. Joan learned her lessons well and was so pious that her friends sometimes teased her about it.

The people of Domremy were intensely loyal to Charles. The village lay in a narrow strip of land hemmed in by Burgundian territory on one side and the duchy of Lorraine on the other. Because the villagers were cut off from the main part of France, they had no protection from the English and Burgundian soldiers, who burned their houses and stole their livestock. The war was very real to Joan, as it was to everyone in Domremy, and they all knew who the enemy was.

One day, when Joan was about thirteen, she was working alone in the garden. At noon, the church bells began to ring. Suddenly she heard a voice. Turning to see who it was, she saw only a brilliant light. Joan did not tell anyone about the voice, and soon it came again. By the third visit, she saw through the light that it was Saint Michael the Archangel. Later, others came to her, especially Saint Margaret and Saint Catherine. She knew them both. There was a statue of Saint Margaret in her parish church. Saint Catherine was the patron saint of the village of Maxey, just across the river. All of them told her to be a good girl and go to church often. She came to love her visions so much that she cried each time they left.

Though Joan was amazed by these visions, she did not question them as we would today. It is important to remember that she lived in the Middle Ages, a time when even educated people believed in fairies, curses, prophecies, witches, and magic. In addition, they were deeply religious and viewed the world not from a scientific point of view but rather a spiritual one. They accepted the unexplainable much more readily than we would today.

As Joan grew older, her visions began telling her distressing things. They spoke of "the great misery there was in the kingdom of France" and said God had a mission for her. She was to leave Domremy and travel through enemy territory to the dauphin at Chinon. Then she must somehow convince him to follow her on the dangerous journey north to the cathedral at Reims, where he would be crowned king. Joan was overwhelmed by this stunning request. She didn't understand how she could fulfill it, for she was just "a poor girl who did not know how to ride or lead in war."

At about this time, her father had a troubling dream in which Joan ran away with soldiers. Jacques took it seriously and began watching her with extra care. He even told her brothers that if Joan ever did such a scandalous thing, they should drown her. On a more loving note, he seems to have decided that marriage was the solution and tried to arrange one. But Joan had made a secret vow never to marry, and she refused, even when the young man took her to court for breaking the promised arrangement. Here is our first glimpse of Joan's strong and steadfast nature.

Joan's voices told her to go to the town of Vaucouleurs and ask the governor for an armed escort to protect her on the journey to Chinon. Conveniently, Joan had a cousin, Jeanne Laxart, who lived near Vaucouleurs. She decided to visit her.

Jeanne's husband, Durand, agreed to take Joan into town and arrange a meeting with the governor, Robert de Baudricourt. This worldly man listened with irritation as she explained that God had sent her there to save France and crown the king. He reacted exactly as you might expect. He told Durand to take the girl back to her father's house "after having thrashed her soundly."

Joan returned home but grew even more determined as the months passed. Once again, Burgundian soldiers threatened her village, sending everyone scurrying to a nearby fortified town, together with their sheep and cattle. When the villagers returned, they found Domremy devastated. Even the church was burned. Three months later, there was more bad news. The great city of Orléans, gateway to loyal France, was surrounded by the English. Now Joan's voices added a new mission: She was to rescue Orléans!

Shortly after her seventeenth birthday, Joan went to see her cousin again. She spent the next month and a half in Vaucouleurs, talking of her quest and pestering the governor. Though he continued to snub her, she began to cause quite a stir among the people. There was a prophecy, widespread at the time, that France would be lost by a woman and saved by a virgin. Everybody knew who the woman was—Queen Isabeau, who had urged the poor mad king to sign away his country. Could it be this pious country girl who was destined to save France?

Among her supporters were two of Baudricourt's soldiers, lively young men of high birth. Perhaps they had a part in convincing the governor to change his mind. Or maybe the French situation had come to seem so hopeless that he was willing to try anything.

But there was one event that may finally have tipped the scales. At their last meeting, Joan had told Baudricourt urgently that, at that very moment, the French were losing another battle to the English, somewhere near Orléans. Sure enough, a few days later, messengers arrived with news of the disastrous battle. It had been just as she had foretold. The governor gave her his blessing.

Joan now began to consider some practical questions, such as how she should dress. A woman riding across dangerous country would be a target for attack. And besides, if she was to ride with an army, she must dress appropriately, in men's clothes. The people of Vaucouleurs soon pitched in, giving her a tunic, hose, boots, and spurs. They also gave her a horse, and Robert de Baudricourt provided a sword. To complete the picture, Joan cut her long hair.

She began now to refer to herself as *la Pucelle,* or "the Maid." This word meant "maiden," or "virgin." Perhaps she hoped to remind people of the prophecy of the virgin who would save France. .

On a cold evening in February, Joan's great journey began. She rode out of the city with an escort of six men, including the two young noblemen who had become her supporters. One of them even paid for the trip. It was three hundred and fifty miles to Chinon, the first part of it through Burgundian territory. To avoid enemy soldiers, they traveled by night, skirting towns and villages. But the dangers didn't end when they reached France. There were still robbers to fear and icy rain-swollen rivers to cross. Joan had never ridden anything but a cart horse around her village, yet she proved to be a natural horsewoman. It's a good thing, too, because for the next two years she would rarely be out of the saddle.

Nearing Chinon, Joan stopped at the little town of Fierbois, where she sent a letter to Charles, saying she would soon arrive and asking for an interview. While there, she prayed at the Chapel of Saint Catherine, a shrine for prisoners of war where the walls were covered with swords, chains, and armor, left there by soldiers grateful for their release. Finally, after eleven days on the road, the small band continued on the short distance to Chinon, arriving there about noon. The people poured out of their houses to stare at them, for the town had talked of little else for days. In fact, by then, the story of the miraculous Maid had already spread throughout France.

It was evening when Joan was escorted up the steep cobblestone streets of Chinon, across the drawbridge, and into the castle grounds. There is a story that as she passed, one of the guards made a crude remark. Joan snapped back that he was mocking God with his insult. "And," she added, "you so near your death!" Within the hour, so the story goes, this same man fell into the moat and drowned. It is easy to imagine how such a tale made the rounds of Chinon before morning.

Entering the grand chamber, Joan was dazzled by a spectacle of color and light. Over three hundred nobles filled the hall, their brilliant silks and velvets glowing in the torchlight. All of them watched her with fascination, for she had boasted that she would know Charles instantly, though she had never seen him. Now she was being tested. Somewhere in that splendid crowd hid the dauphin. His clothes did not set him apart from the others. Nor did he look kingly, with his large nose and small, sleepy eyes. Yet Joan headed straight for Charles as if he were an old and familiar friend. "God give you life, gentle king," she said. He answered, "I am not the king, Joan. There is the king!" and he pointed to another man. But she was not fooled. "By God, gentle prince, it is you and none other!"

Now Joan got straight to the point. She said her voices had revealed that Charles was indeed the "true heir of France and the king's son." But until he had been anointed with sacred oil and given the blessing of God, Charles would never truly be king, and that was why she had come. Joan would lead him to Reims, where all French kings had been crowned for almost a thousand years.

Then, withdrawing from the others, Joan gave Charles a sign to prove she came from God. No one really knows what the sign was, but witnesses said that as she spoke, his face grew radiant and he was much changed.

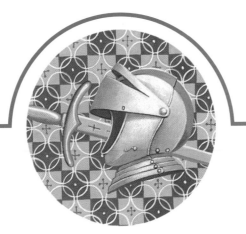

Before the king could ride north to be crowned, however, something had to be done about the English still surrounding Orléans. Not only could they threaten the king's safe passage to Reims, but with the French army gone north with the king, the English might choose to cross the Loire and capture the French stronghold in the south. Joan was anxious to get started.

Charles, on the other hand, was always cautious. Before he put French troops in Joan's hands, he wanted to be sure her voices came from God and not from the devil. He took her to the town of Poitiers and asked the council of church scholars there to examine her. Week after week, the questioning dragged on. Joan grew increasingly restless. Could she not give them some sign, they asked, that her mission was a holy one? Exasperated, she gave her famous reply, "I have not come to Poitiers to make signs! Take me to Orléans, and I will show you the sign for which I have been sent!"

In the end, the church fathers found nothing but good in her. Their advice was that, considering "the peril in which the town of Orléans stood…, the king could well use her help."

Preparations now began in earnest. Charles raised an army with the financial help of his mother-in-law. Joan was given a suit of armor, described in the records as *"à blanc."* This did not mean, as some have supposed, that it was white, but that the armor was plain, having no ornamentation or coat of arms.

Joan already had a sword, but there was another one she wanted. She sent a message to Fierbois, where she had stopped to pray at the Chapel of Saint Catherine. She asked if she might have the sword they would find buried behind the altar there. Though no one had ever heard of such a sword, they began digging just the same. To everyone's amazement, they found it. It came to be called the "miraculous sword of Fierbois."

Much as she loved her sword, she loved her standard more. This banner was always carried ahead of her by a standard-bearer, to show the soldiers where she was. It had great symbolic meaning to Joan. She thought it protected her from ever killing anyone in battle, a tender concern for someone going to war.

The people of Orléans rejoiced: An army was coming to their rescue, led by the saintly Maid of God. The truth was that Joan was not really the commander, only one of the captains. But she was the true heart and soul of the army, and she looked after its spiritual well-being. She made all the soldiers go to confession and would not allow them to swear. Joan told the men to be merciful conquerors, never burning villages or stealing from the people. They must do nothing to displease the King of Heaven because, she said, the army would fight the battle, but God would grant the victory.

Among the men who rode with Joan to Orléans were two who had traveled a long way to join the army of the Maid. They were Joan's brothers, Pierre and Jean, once ordered to drown her if she ever ran off with soldiers!

Under normal circumstances, the duke of Orléans would have led the defense of his city. But he could not do so now, for he was a prisoner of war in England. Instead, it was his half-brother, Jean, the count of Dunois, who would be in command. As the army neared the city, he rode out to greet it.

Though he and Joan would soon become friends, they got off to a bad start. At this first meeting Joan lost her temper. She had expected to attack the English right away. But Dunois explained that the fighting was to be put off until more soldiers arrived. Joan rudely accused him of deceiving her. One can only imagine what he thought of her insolence.

The army, with cartloads of food and a herd of cattle, successfully entered the city. This was possible because the English had too few men to surround Orléans completely, leaving the east gate unchallenged much of the time. Though it was late in the evening, the streets were filled with joyous citizens. They cheered as Joan passed by, reaching out to touch her. A spirit of hope was in the air.

Other English forts

Saint-Loup

ORLÉANS

The Tourelles

LOIRE R.

Les Augustins   Saint Jean le Blanc

While waiting for reinforcements, Joan sent several letters to the English, urging them to go back to their own country and threatening great peril if they did not. Joan dictated these letters and someone else wrote them for her, since she never learned to read, nor could she write anything but her own name, which she spelled Jehanne. The English, not surprisingly, thought her letters were total rubbish and responded that Joan ought to go home and mind the cows.

Still determined to prevent bloodshed if she could, Joan decided on a more personal appeal. She rode through the south gate of the city and out onto the bridge that spanned the Loire River. Guarding the far side of the bridge was a stone fort called the Tourelles, now in the hands of the English. To keep them from crossing, the French had destroyed a section of the bridge. Now, from the Orléans side, Joan shouted across that the English should abandon the fort immediately and save their lives. They hooted back, "Cowgirl!"

The French high command didn't take her very seriously either. They saw her as a kind of mascot, or good-luck charm. One officer called her "a little saucebox of low birth." When reinforcements arrived and Dunois began planning his assault, he didn't bother to include Joan. The next day, the army rode out to attack the fortress at Saint-Loup while Joan was taking a nap. Suddenly she woke in a state of agitation, crying out that French blood was being spilled. Arming quickly, she hurried to join the battle. Things had been going poorly for the French, but when the soldiers saw her, they gave a great cheer. With the army's spirits lifted, the tide turned, and Saint-Loup fell.

Two days later, the English abandoned a second fort, south of the river, and fled to the fortified abbey of the Augustins. The French expected no more action that day, so they turned back toward Orléans. Suddenly, the English came darting out of the abbey to attack the unsuspecting French from the rear. Seeing the danger, Joan and a daring captain called La Hire set their lances and, all by themselves, charged the English. Inspired by their courage, the French turned and joined the charge, taking the fort of the Augustins.

ORLÉANS

Bridge

Broken section

The Tourelles

Drawbridge

Fortification

Les Augustins

Joan was often able to predict future events, and that night she told her priest what would happen the next day. She would be wounded "above the breast" but would survive, and the French would take the Tourelles.

The battle began in the early morning of May 7, 1429, with an assault on the fortification that guarded the Tourelles. Joan was the first to set a ladder against the wall, but neither she nor any of the others succeeded in getting over. They climbed beneath a rain of arrows, only to be repelled at the top by English swords and battle-axes. About midday Joan was struck by an arrow in the shoulder, just as she had predicted. Her men carried her to safety, where, it is said, she pulled the arrow out herself. She rested only a short time, then returned to the action.

Night came, and after thirteen hours of fierce fighting, the men were exhausted. But Joan was sure of victory and begged Dunois to keep trying. He agreed, and while the men rested and ate, Joan found a quiet place to pray.

When she returned, Joan picked up her standard and carried it to the edge of the moat, where all could see her. The sight inspired the French to make one last, ferocious attack. By then, the English were convinced that Joan was a witch and was using sorcery on them. Their defenses broke down, allowing the French to pour over the walls unhindered. The terrified English hurried toward the drawbridge leading to the Tourelles, unaware that the French had stationed a boat underneath it that they set on fire. As the English crossed the bridge, it caught fire and collapsed. Unable to swim in their armor, the English—including Glasdale, the commander—were drowned.

Meanwhile, the citizens of Orléans spanned the broken part of the bridge with ladders, boards, and gutter pipes. Over this wobbly structure the citizens crossed to attack the Tourelles from the rear, setting it on fire with flaming arrows.

The victory was so stunning that on the following morning, the English commander Lord Talbot abandoned all the remaining forts around Orléans. From that time on, the people of Orléans have celebrated every seventh of May with festivities and torchlight processions in memory of that glorious day.

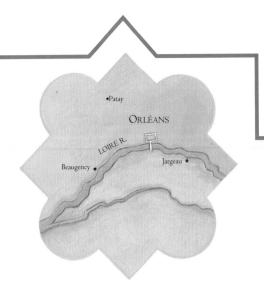

The next morning, Joan rode to the dauphin's castle. Charles was so pleased to see her that one witness thought "he would readily have kissed her in his joy." She stayed there for almost two weeks while the king and his counselors debated their next move. "Noble dauphin," she pleaded, "do not hold such long council, but go to Reims as soon as possible and receive your worthy crown!"

Eventually, she won him over, and the army set off to clear the way for the march to Reims. The command for this expedition went to the duke of Alençon, who had also fought at Orléans. Joan admired him greatly, for his charm as much as his courage. She called him her *beau duc,* her "handsome duke."

The Loire campaign was as short as it was successful. Over the period of one remarkable week, the French army captured several occupied towns along the Loire. The first to fall was Jargeau, where the English had retreated from Orléans. Next, Beaugency surrendered. By then, however, Lord Talbot's English forces had been reinforced by the army of Sir John Fastolf (later immortalized in two plays by Shakespeare as the colorful Sir John Falstaff). This combined army was now advancing toward the French. Alençon, worried that they might be outmanned, asked Joan's advice. "Do you all have good spurs?" she asked.

In disbelief, the men cried, "Are we going to turn our backs on them?"

Of course they were not. "You will need good spurs," Joan said, "to run after them."

And, indeed, on that day in the woods of Patay, according to Dunois's estimation, more than four thousand English were killed or captured while the French lost only three men. Lord Talbot himself was taken prisoner.

At last the time had come to go to Reims. As the royal army moved north, they found that Joan's reputation had cleared the way for them. Towns opened their gates without a fight. Throughout the occupied territory, enemy soldiers began to desert in fear of the Maid. Two weeks later, Charles arrived unscathed at the gates of Reims, where the people offered him their "full and entire obedience as their sovereign."

The king and his army reached Reims on a Saturday, and it was traditional to hold coronations on Sundays. Since the people didn't want to feed the entire army for a week, they began hurried preparations to crown Charles the next day.

At nine o'clock on the morning of July 17, 1429, the grand procession made its way to Reims Cathedral for the coronation, a ceremony that would last most of the day. It began with prayers and music. Then, with his hand on the Bible, Charles swore an oath to uphold the Catholic faith, defend the Church, and rule his kingdom with justice and mercy. Then the king was knighted by the duke of Alençon.

Next, the archbishop took a golden needle and withdrew a drop of holy oil from a sacred vial. This vial was almost a thousand years old, dating back to the baptism of Clovis, the first Christian king of France. Legend held that, on that occasion, it was brought down from heaven by a dove. Since then, all French kings had been anointed with its holy oil, as Charles now was, on his head, chest, back, shoulders, and elbows.

Charles then received the scepter, a symbol of authority, which he held in his right hand, and the rod of justice, which he held in his left. The belt and spurs of chivalry were strapped on. Finally, the archbishop laid the crown of France on the head of this timid and homely young man for whom so many had fought and died. Joan knelt proudly and wept with joy. In her hand she held her standard. Later, when asked why it had been given such a place of prominence in the ceremony, she answered, "It had borne the burden; it deserved the honor."

The king later rewarded Joan by raising her family to the nobility. He also granted the only favor she asked, that her little village be forever exempt from taxes.

That day was the finest moment of her life. And there to witness it were her mother and father and two brothers. Several others came from Domremy, too. Even Durand Laxart was there to see the grand climax of that journey he had helped her begin only six months before.

Now the great moment of decision arrived on which so much depended. Joan's miraculous victories were the talk of France. Charles had been properly crowned at Reims. Throughout the north, cities that had long lain under Anglo-Burgundian control were ready to submit to him. The army, under the command of the duke of Alençon, was eager to fight. Had Charles been a bolder man, he would have seized this moment to take Paris and drive the English out of France altogether.

But Charles still hoped to end the war by winning the duke of Burgundy away from his English alliance. So now, without telling Joan, he agreed to a truce of fifteen days, after which Burgundy promised to give up Paris. Of course, he did not. He was just stalling for time, well aware that thirty-five hundred knights and archers had already left England to reinforce Paris. By the time Charles reluctantly agreed to attack, three precious weeks had been wasted.

This was to prove far more difficult than the battle of Orléans had been. Paris was well fortified, and the walls were protected by a moat. Before the French could even set up their ladders, they had to pile bundles of branches into the water to get across. Joan, ever hoping to prevent bloodshed, called up to the defenders, urging them to yield quickly or face the consequences. An English archer, seeing what an easy target she made, called back, "Here's for you!" and let loose an arrow from his crossbow, piercing her thigh. Joan watched helplessly as, once again, the archer took aim and her standard-bearer fell. Her banner, which had borne such burdens and won such honor, now lay in the dust.

Joan was carried from the field, and the French withdrew for the night. The following morning, before the battle could resume, a message came from the king. He ordered them to abandon the fight and return to the town of Saint-Denis, where he was in residence. This was a terrible blow, but there was still hope, for Alençon had a backup plan.

Earlier, he had ordered a bridge to be built across the Seine at Saint-Denis. They would retreat, but then they would cross the river and come around for a surprise attack from the south. Imagine their dismay when they learned that the king had ordered the bridge destroyed! Beguiled by Burgundy's promise of new peace talks, Charles had decided to retreat. So the army of the king left Saint-Denis and headed south—"without," it was recorded, "paying their lodging."

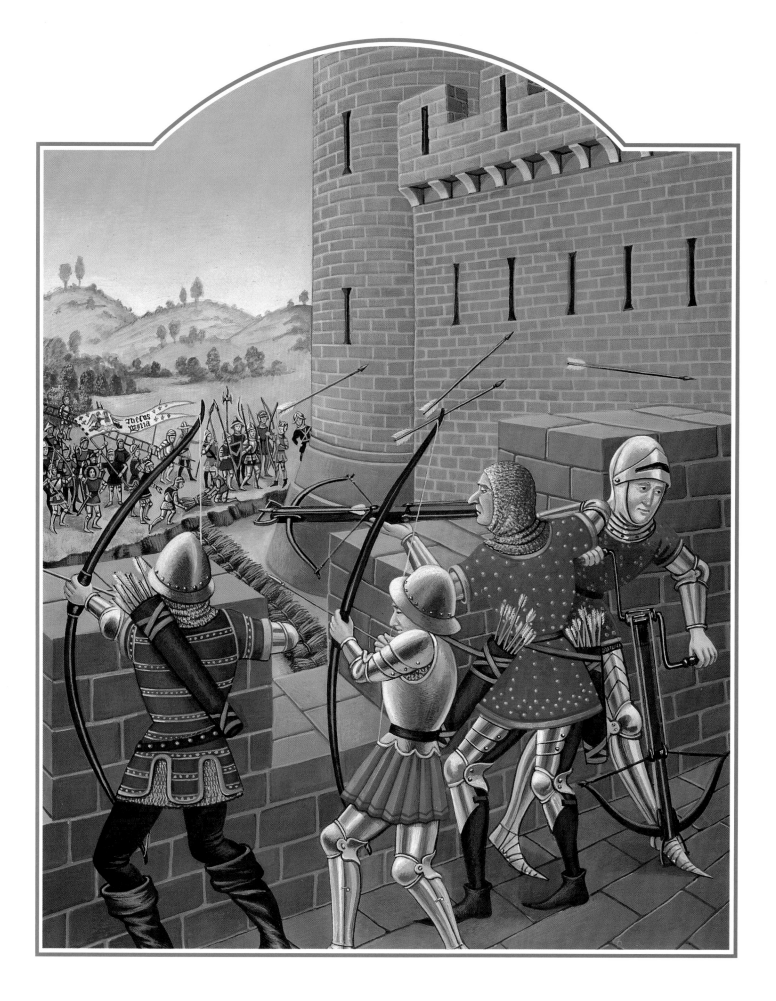

Charles disbanded his army and spent the next six months hoping that the duke of Burgundy would play fair this time. While Charles did nothing, a thousand more soldiers crossed the English Channel to take back everything he had gained. At the same time, Burgundy used the threat of peace talks to goad the English into buying his loyalty with more money and territory. Joan did not wait for Charles to realize his mistake. She joined a small band of freelance soldiers and headed north to fight.

At the beginning of her mission, Joan's voices had told her that she would last only a year, perhaps a little more. Now, the voices said, her time was up. She would soon be captured. With this new weight on her young shoulders, Joan learned that the duke of Burgundy had laid siege to the important city of Compiègne. As part of a truce, Charles had given the city back to Burgundy, but the people had refused, saying they would "rather lose their lives, and that of their wives and children, than to expose them to the mercy of the duke." Deeply moved by this story, Joan rushed to their defense. With about four hundred men, she slipped through enemy lines by night and entered the city.

The next afternoon, Joan rode out the north gate with a small force of soldiers to attack a Burgundian encampment on the far side of the drawbridge. The enemy, caught by surprise, retreated hastily. As the French galloped in pursuit, they suddenly found themselves ambushed and in danger of being cut off from the town. Joan tried valiantly to convince her men to take heart and fight, but they had already turned and were racing back, the Burgundians at their heels. The governor of Compiègne watched with horror as the pursuers came closer and closer to the bridge. When he could wait no longer, for fear of losing the town, the governor ordered the drawbridge raised and the gate closed.

Joan, who had been guarding the retreat, was shut out. Soldiers surrounded her, shouting wildly, "Yield to me! Yield to me!" Then an archer, "a rough man and sour," grabbed hold of her cloak and pulled Joan from her horse. She was now a prisoner.

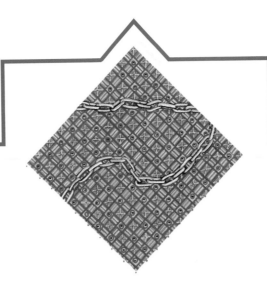

Joan was a great prize, and the English wanted her badly. They had come to believe that "they would never in her lifetime win glory or prosperity in deeds of war." Now the English were determined to put an end to her. Over the next few weeks, they pressured the duke of Burgundy to turn her over. Burgundy finally accepted an offer of ten thousand francs ransom, plus an additional six thousand for the men who had captured her.

Though she was ransomed by the English, Joan would be tried by the Inquisition. This was a special court appointed to deal with heretics, people who opposed the established beliefs of the Church. She was accused of many things, but the case boiled down to two charges. The first was that she dressed in men's clothes, which was considered an "abomination to God." The second was that she claimed God guided her personally, through voices and visitations. This was a sin because only the Church, as God's representative on earth, could tell ordinary Christians what He wanted them to do. But the English were more interested in the political angle: If Joan was found guilty of witchcraft and sorcery, then Charles, by association, would be discredited.

When Joan learned from her jailers that she had been sold to the English, she grew distraught. In her despair, she threw herself from the prison tower, a fall of sixty or seventy feet. Hours later, the guards found her lying unconscious in a ditch. It was incredible that she survived at all. More amazing still, she was not even injured, though for a few days she was unable to eat.

Joan had been captured in the spring. From her various prisons she watched summer come, then fade into autumn. Finally, just after Christmas, she was brought to the city of Rouen for her trial. Joan expected to be kept in a church prison, guarded by priests and nuns, as was customary in religious trials. Instead, the English put her in a dark cell in the castle of Rouen, where she was put in chains and guarded by brutish English soldiers.

Joan's case would be decided by two judges. Pierre Cauchon, bishop of Beauvais, really ran the trial. The other judge was Jean Lemaître, deputy inquisitor of France. He either disapproved of or was not interested in the proceedings, for he rarely attended the court, and when he did, said nothing. The judges were advised by as many as sixty eminent scholars of theology and church law. Against the weight of all this knowledge and authority stood a peasant girl of nineteen, unable to read or write and without a lawyer to help her.

During the trial, three notaries recorded everything that was said. These notes were later translated into Latin and copied in formal handwriting. This transcript still exists today, giving us an accurate picture of the proceedings. We can see, for example, how the questioners tried to confuse Joan by jumping around from subject to subject or interrupting her in the middle of answers. They frequently repeated questions, in hopes that she would contradict herself, and tried to trip her up on points of theology.

To their surprise, they discovered that this ignorant girl was not easily intimidated and was remarkably clever in her answers. They asked, for example, if she was in a state of grace. This was a trick question, because if she said yes, she would be claiming knowledge belonging only to God. If she said no, that meant she was in a state of sin. With characteristic common sense she answered, "If I am not, may God put me there; if I am, may God keep me there." The court, according to one witness, was "stupefied."

Joan was also quick with a bold and saucy answer. "Does God hate the English?" she was asked. "Of the love or hate which God has for the English…," she replied, "I know nothing; but I do know that they will be driven out of France, except for those who will die here, and that God will send victory to the French over the English."

Cauchon had promised a "beautiful trial," one in which all the correct procedures were followed. In truth, it was just the opposite. Anyone sympathetic to Joan was sent away, documents were falsified, and the judges were hardly impartial. There was never any doubt that she would be found guilty. Still, the trial was not swift or ruthless enough to suit the English, for the goal of the Church was to save souls, not to burn heretics. Church officials spent weeks urging her to give up her false beliefs and win forgiveness. They even threatened her with torture, but Joan stood firm. Cauchon finally declared the trial finished.

The next day, Joan was led through a jostling crowd to the walled cemetery of the Abbey of Saint-Ouen to hear the verdict. First, she was subjected to a sermon in which she was berated as a "useless, infamous, dishonored woman" and King Charles was called a heretic. Ever loyal, Joan broke in to defend the king. He was the "noblest Christian of all," she declared. "Make her be quiet," said Cauchon.

The verdict followed. Cauchon declared Joan a heretic, cut off forever from the Church and abandoned to English justice. At that moment, she panicked. Her voices had assured her that she would be rescued. But Charles had neither offered to pay her ransom nor tried to exchange her for English prisoners. No hosts of angels had come to open her prison door. She knew, suddenly, that she was about to die. Terrified of the fire, she broke down and signed the document that had been prepared. She agreed to put on women's clothes and to obey the Church in all things.

The English were furious, and some began throwing stones. They had spent a lot of money for her ransom and more on the trial, and now she had escaped with her life. But Cauchon reassured them; they would catch her yet.

Joan did not win her freedom by repenting. Instead, she was sentenced to life in prison, where she would live "on the bread of sorrow and the water of affliction." She begged to be moved to a church prison, but even this was denied. Cauchon responded coldly, "Take her to where you found her." And so the guards returned Joan to her cell, where, to mark her penitence, they shaved off her hair. Then they put her back in chains.

Joan was given a dress to wear, but men's clothing was left in her cell, as if her captors were daring her to put it back on. Indeed, four days later, Joan defied the Church and doomed herself by once again dressing as a man. She supposedly told Cauchon that she had done it willingly, preferring death to life in an English prison. Others explained it differently: either that the guards forced her into it by taking her dress away or that she thought men's clothes, with their leggings and tight laces, protected her from the crude advances of her jailers. Either way, as Joan said several times, it would not have happened had they put her in a church prison.

Early in the morning of May 30, 1431, two priests came to Joan's cell to hear her last confession and to tell her that, within the hour, she was to be burned at the stake. Joan burst into tears. It was such a dreadful way to die!

Joan was to go to her death in proper women's clothes, but on her head she was forced to wear a tall paper cap with the words *heretic, relapsed, apostate, idolatress* written on it. Under close guard, she was brought to the Old Market Square, where a restless crowd awaited the spectacle. There, frightened and heartsick, she endured yet another sermon. Then she knelt and began to pray aloud, begging God's mercy and forgiving those who had wronged her. Her terrible grief and devout words moved the crowd so deeply that "even several Englishmen...most bitterly wept at it." Others with harder hearts grew impatient. "Do you mean to have us dine here?" one shouted.

Finally, for the second time, Cauchon pronounced Joan cast out of the Catholic Church and turned over to the state for justice. Then, without waiting for the sheriff of Rouen to sentence her, the guards hastily took her to the scaffold and bound her to the stake.

Joan asked for a cross, so someone in the crowd tied two sticks together for her. A sympathetic priest hurried into the church and brought out the crucifix, which he held up to comfort her in her last, dreadful moments. When it was all over, the English had her ashes gathered and thrown into the Seine.

Many who were there that day went home unnerved by what they had seen. The executioner said he feared for his soul. Even the secretary to the king of England wept. "We are all lost," he cried, "for we have burnt a saint!"

After Joan's death, the tide began to turn in France. When little King Henry VI was brought to Paris to be crowned king of France (Reims was still controlled by the French), the duke of Burgundy did not attend. Instead, he began negotiations with Charles for a real truce. In 1435, Burgundy acknowledged his old enemy as king of France, and peace was concluded between them. The war dragged on for another eighteen years, but by 1453, the English were gone and the war was over. By then, Charles was well on his way to becoming the good and serious king Joan had always believed him to be.

With Rouen back in French hands, Charles finally had access to the transcript of Joan's trial. Though he had not tried to save her, the king now set about clearing her name. A royal commission concluded that the trial had been fraudulent and driven by political aims. Since Joan had been convicted by the Inquisition, only the pope could order a Trial of Rehabilitation and only the Inquisition could hear it. An official request was presented to Pope Calixtus III in the name of Joan's elderly mother and two brothers. It begins, touchingly, "I had a daughter," and tells how good and devoted Joan was. Although Joan had never done anything to deserve it, the letter went on, her enemies "without any assistance given to her innocence...did condemn her...and put her to death very cruelly by fire."

The request set in motion a serious investigation in which one hundred and fifteen witnesses were examined. The judges traveled to Domremy, where they heard from Joan's childhood friends. They went to Vaucouleurs, where Durand Laxart told how he had taken Joan to speak with the governor. Baudricourt was no longer alive, but the two noblemen who had first supported her were still there. They told the court how they had traveled with Joan to Chinon to see the king all those years before. In Paris, the judges questioned the count of Dunois and Joan's *beau duc,* Alençon, who both described the battle of Orléans, the Loire campaign, and the grand march to Reims. At Rouen they got a chance to read the original transcript and interviewed, among others, one of the notaries and several of the advisers from the first trial.

A hearing was held at which anyone who opposed the rehabilitation of Joan the Maid could come and speak. No one did.

Finally, on July 7, 1456, more than six years after Charles began to look into the matter, and twenty-five years after Joan's death, a second verdict was announced. "The trial and sentence being tainted with fraud," the conviction of heresy was considered "null, invalid, worthless, without effect and annihilated," and Joan was "washed clean…absolutely."

The document was read at the cemetery of Saint-Ouen, where Joan had recanted out of fear. The next day, it was read again in the Old Market, where she gave up her life. There, the king erected a stone cross in her memory.

In 1920, almost five hundred years after her death, Joan of Arc was made a saint by the Catholic Church.

The transcript of Joan's trial for heresy is much more than just the record of a judicial proceeding; it is the autobiography of Joan of Arc. Through her answers, in her own simple words, she gives us a first-person account of her childhood, her visions, and her extraordinary career. In the same way, the Trial of Rehabilitation can be read as Joan's biography, as told by people who were there to see and participate in the great events of her life. Because of these two remarkable documents, we know more about Joan of Arc than about any other woman who lived before modern times. All of the quotes in this book were taken from the transcripts of the trials.

But now that we have the story, what are we to make of it? How, in reading a historical account that is based on hard facts and documentary evidence, are we supposed to make sense of miraculous visions and voices? Depending on our point of view, we can account for them in one of three ways. First, they were exactly what Joan said they were: divine revelations. Second, they were hallucinations produced by some illness of mind or body. And third, seeing the terrible state of her country and having heard the prophecy about the young girl who would save France, she began to wish, and then actually to believe, that she was the chosen one. To this day, however, no historian has been able to do more than spin the occasional theory. Sometimes, in studying history, we have to accept what we know and let the rest remain a mystery.

Bibliography

Barrett, W. P. *The Trial of Jeanne d'Arc.* London: George Routledge & Sons, 1931.

Gies, Frances. *Joan of Arc: The Legend and the Reality.* New York: Harper & Row, 1981.

Lightbody, Charles Wayland. *The Judgments of Joan: Joan of Arc, a Study in Cultural History.* Cambridge, MA: Harvard University Press, 1961.

Michelet, Jules. *Joan of Arc.* Translated, with an introduction by Albert Guerard. Ann Arbor: University of Michigan Press, 1957.

Pernoud, Regine. *Joan of Arc: By Herself and Her Witnesses.* New York: Stein and Day, 1966.

Sackville-West, V. *Saint Joan of Arc.* Boston: G. K. Hall & Company, 1984.

Trask, Willard. *Joan of Arc: Self Portrait.* New York: Stackpole Sons, 1936.

Warner, Marina. *Joan of Arc: The Image of Female Heroism.* New York: Knopf, 1981.

Recommended for Younger Readers

Banfield, Susan. *Joan of Arc.* New York: Chelsea House, 1988.

Boutet De Monvel, Maurice. *Joan of Arc.* New York: Viking, 1980. (Reprint of original 1896 French edition.)

Brooks, Polly Schoyer. *Beyond the Myth: The Story of Joan of Arc.* New York: Lippincott, 1990.

Christopher, Tracy. *Joan of Arc: Soldier Saint.* New York: Chelsea House, 1993.

Garden, Nancy. *Dove and Sword: A Novel of Joan of Arc.* New York: Farrar, Straus & Giroux, 1995. (Fictionalized)

Twain, Mark. *Personal Recollections of Joan of Arc.* New York: Harper & Row, 1886. (Fictionalized)

Williams, Jay. *Joan of Arc.* New York: American Heritage Publishing Company, 1963.